# MASTERWORK CLASSICS DUETS

## A GRADED COLLECTION OF PIANO DUETS BY MASTER COMPOSERS

### SELECTED AND EDITED BY GAYLE KOWALCHYK, E. L. LANCASTER, AND JANE MAGRATH

## CONTENTS

Copyright © 2013 by Alfred Music
All rights reserved
ISBN-10: 0-7390-9513-7
ISBN-13: 978-0-7390-9513-3

*Cover art:* Copyright © Planet Art

# Sonatina in D Minor

from *Pleasures of Youth*

SECONDO

Anton Diabelli (1781–1858)
Op. 163, No. 6

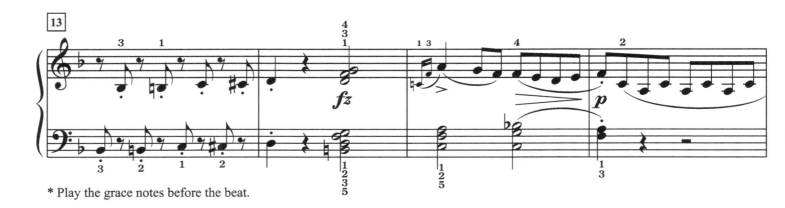

* Play the grace notes before the beat.

# Sonatina in D Minor
## from *Pleasures of Youth*
### PRIMO

Anton Diabelli (1781–1858)
Op. 163, No. 6

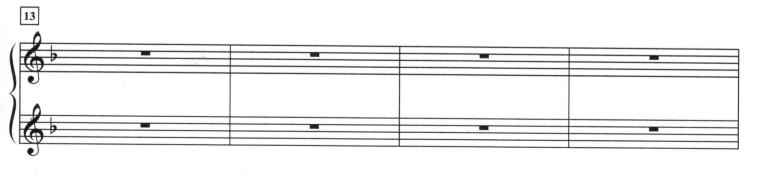

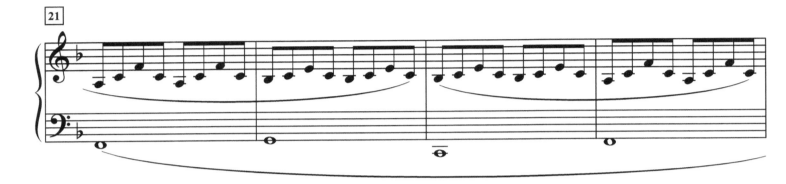

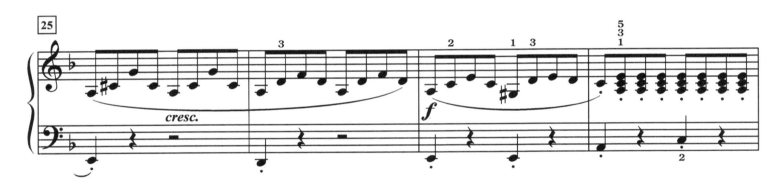

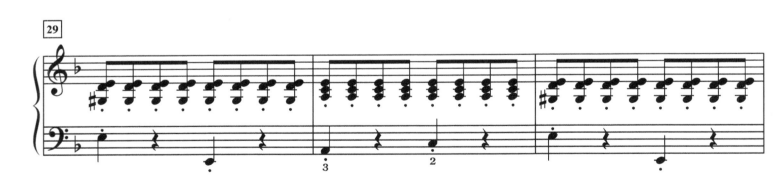

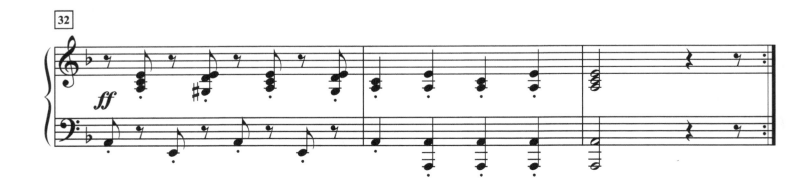

* Play the grace notes before the beat.

SECONDO

# Sonatina in C Major

## Romance

### from *Pleasures of Youth*

#### SECONDO

Anton Diabelli (1781–1858)
Op. 163, No. 1

# Sonatina in C Major
### Romance
from *Pleasures of Youth*
#### PRIMO

Anton Diabelli (1781–1858)
Op. 163, No. 1

Andantino

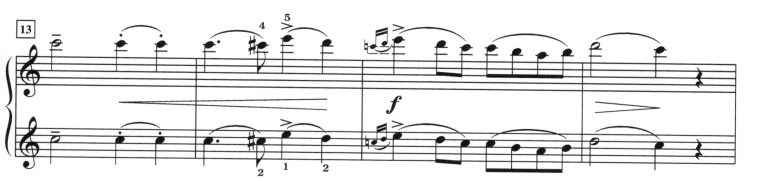

\* Play the grace notes before the beat.

# Sonatina in C Major

## Rondo

### from *Pleasures of Youth*

#### SECONDO

Anton Diabelli (1781–1858)
Op. 163, No. 1

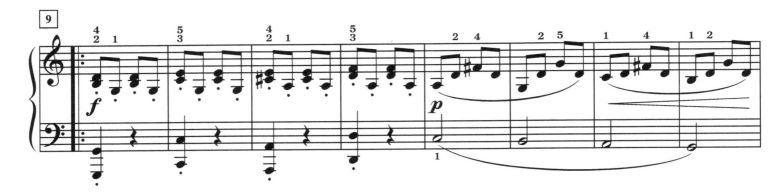

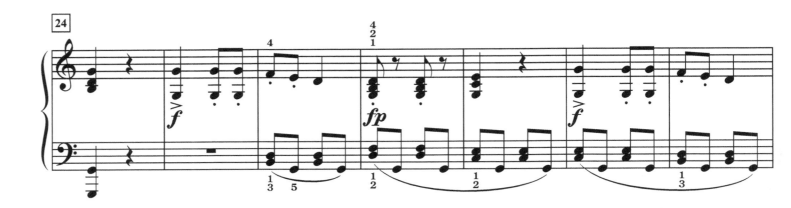

# Sonatina in C Major

### Rondo
### from *Pleasures of Youth*

PRIMO

Anton Diabelli (1781–1858)
Op. 163, No. 1

**Allegro vivace**
*RH one octave higher than written throughout*

\* Play the grace notes before the beat.

# Allegretto in G Major

## SECONDO

Carl Czerny (1791–1857)
Op. 824, No. 18

# Allegretto in G Major

## PRIMO

Carl Czerny (1791–1857)
Op. 824, No. 18

Student
# Tarantella
from *Daily Studies on Harmonized Scales*
### SECONDO

Ignaz Moscheles (1794–1870)
Op. 107, No. 15

Teacher
# Tarantella
from *Daily Studies on Harmonized Scales*
PRIMO

Ignaz Moscheles (1794–1870)
Op. 107, No. 15

# Mysterious Story

## SECONDO

Theodor Kirchner (1823–1903)
Op. 57, No. 2

# Mysterious Story

PRIMO

Theodor Kirchner (1823–1903)
Op. 57, No. 2

# Immortelle No. 1

## SECONDO

Fritz Spindler
(1817–1905)

Semplice

# Immortelle No. 1

### PRIMO

Fritz Spindler
(1817–1905)

# Immortelle No. 2

## SECONDO

Fritz Spindler
(1817–1905)

Piacevole (Graceful)

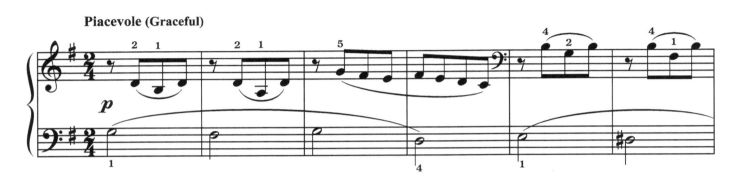

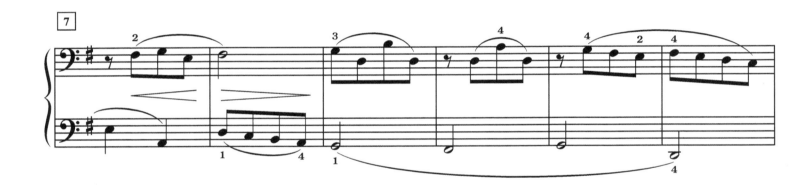

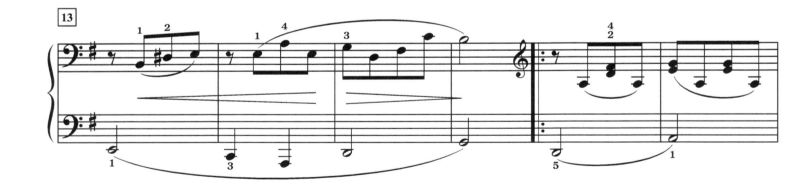

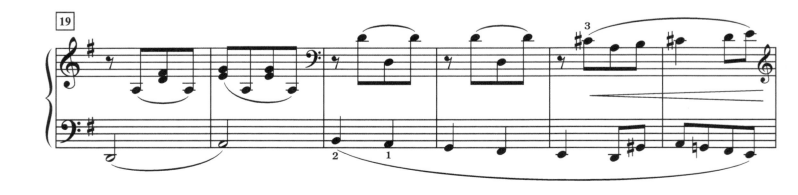

# Immortelle No. 2

PRIMO

Fritz Spindler
(1817–1905)

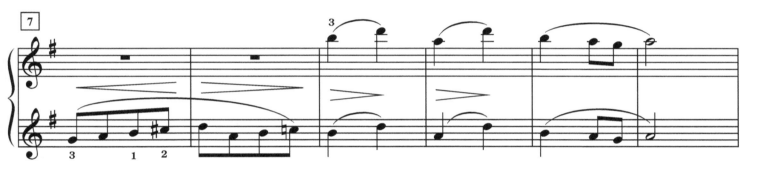

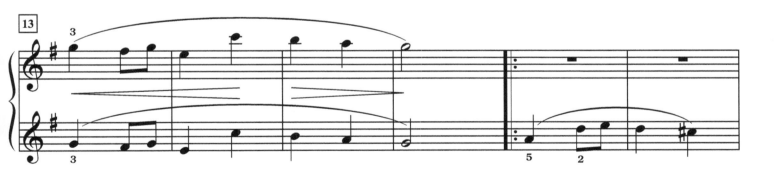

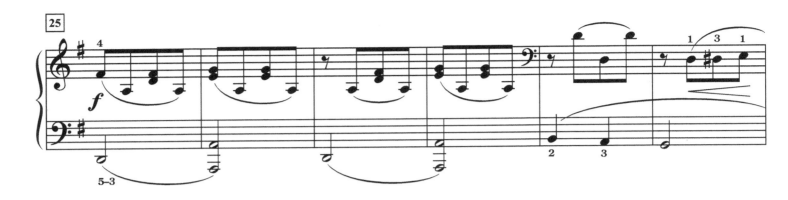

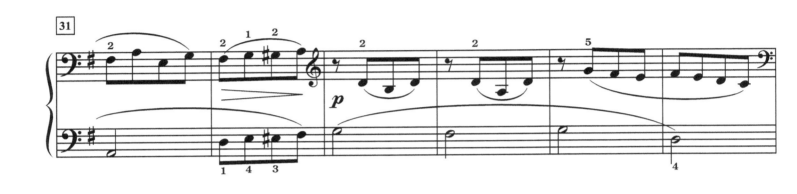

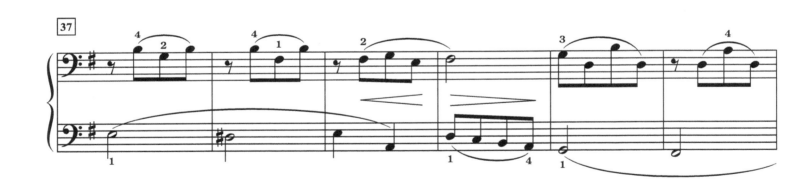

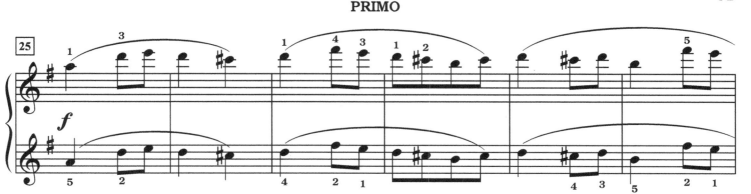

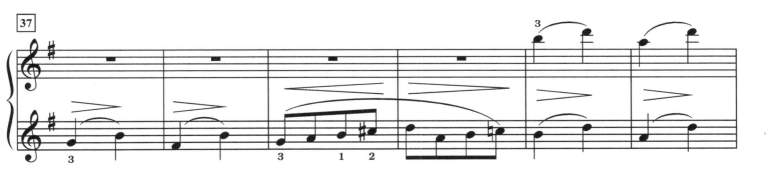

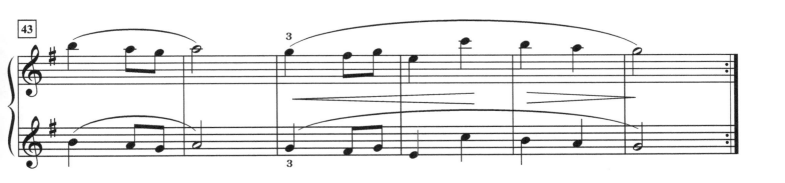

# Immortelle No. 3

## SECONDO

Fritz Spindler
(1817–1905)

Innocente (Innocent, simple)

# Immortelle No. 3

### PRIMO

Fritz Spindler
(1817–1905)

# Immortelle No. 4

## SECONDO

Fritz Spindler
(1817–1905)

Con devozione (With devotion and sincerity)

# Immortelle No. 4

## PRIMO

Fritz Spindler
(1817–1905)

Con devozione (With devotion and sincerity)

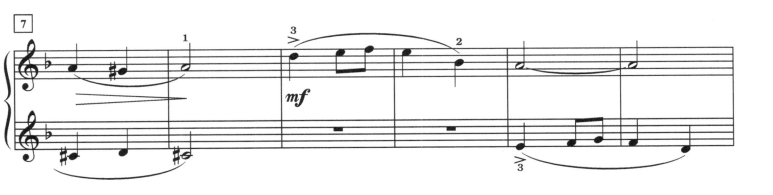

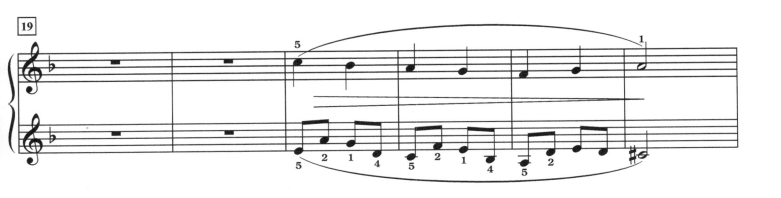

# Immortelle No. 5

**SECONDO**

Fritz Spindler
(1817–1905)

# Immortelle No. 5

## PRIMO

Fritz Spindler
(1817–1905)

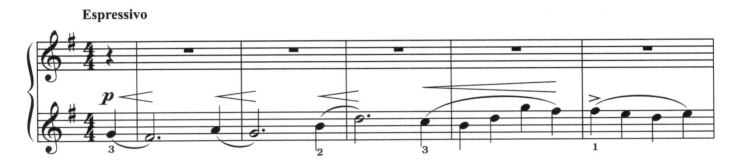

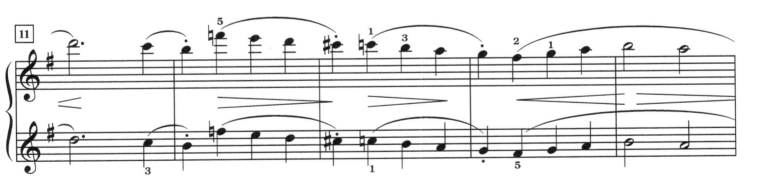

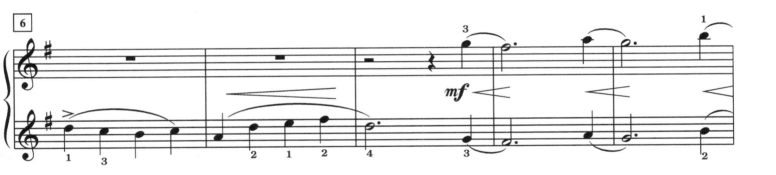

SECONDO

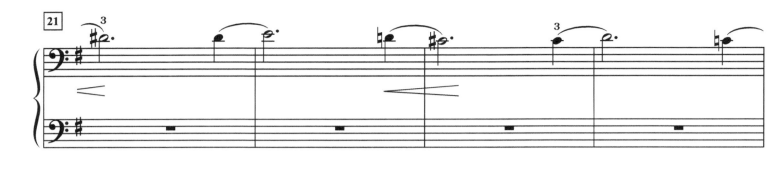

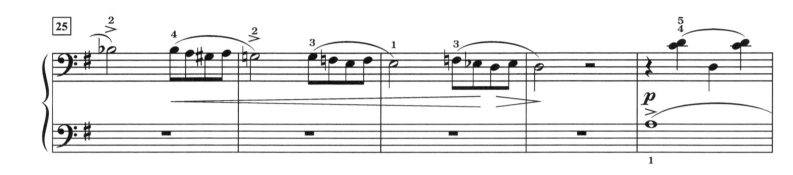

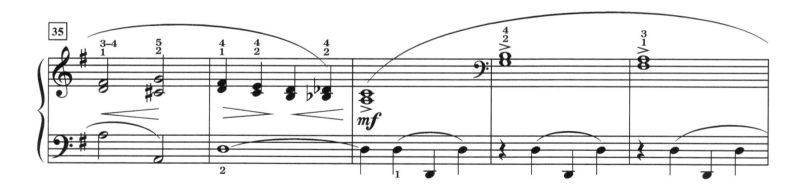

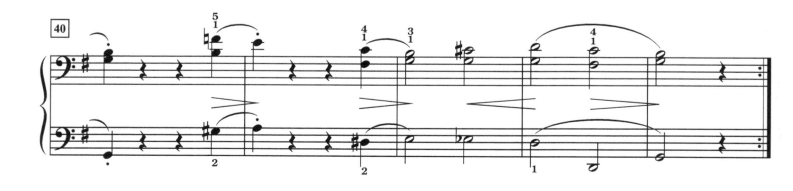

# Katy-dids

## SECONDO

Amy Beach (1867–1944)
Op. 47, No. 4

Vivace

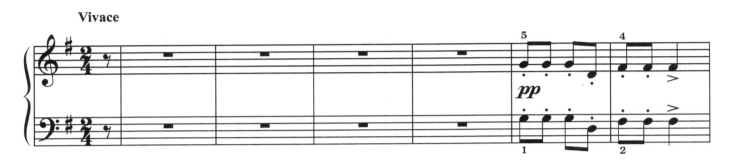

*pp*

*sempre staccato*

*poco a poco cresc.*

# Katy-dids

## PRIMO

Amy Beach (1867–1944)
Op. 47, No. 4

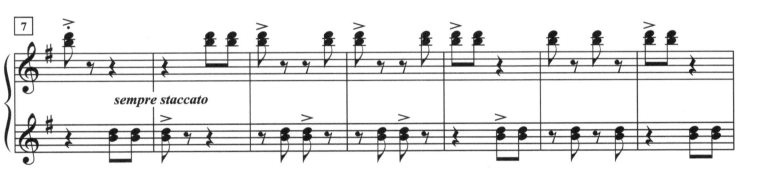

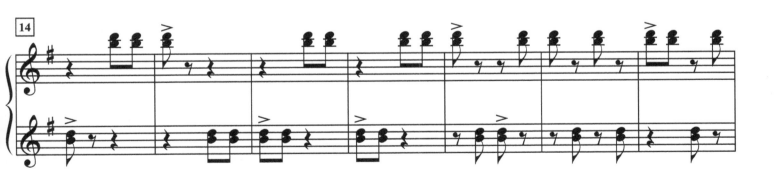

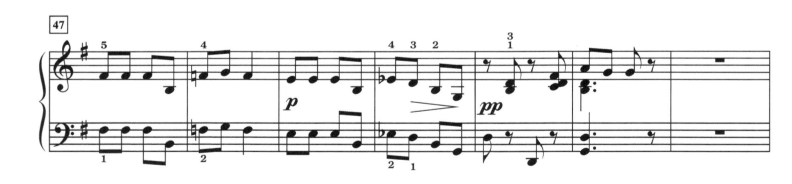

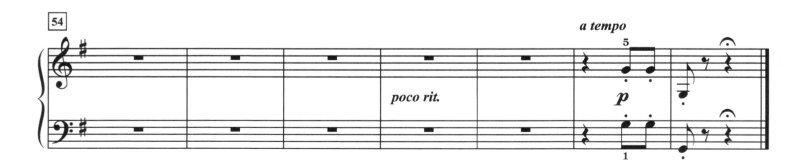

# Andante

from *Five Easy Pieces*

SECONDO

Igor Stravinsky
(1882–1971)

# Andante

## from *Five Easy Pieces*

### PRIMO

Igor Stravinsky
(1882–1971)

ABOUT THIS COLLECTION

This collection contains duets written by teachers and composers who lived in the 18th, 19th, and 20th centuries. They can be used with students of all ages. To facilitate ease in reading the score by young students, the *primo* and *secondo* parts are on separate pages. Each duet has been carefully edited and fingered for performance ease. No pedal indications have been given as all these duets can be successfully performed without pedal. Some teachers may choose to add pedal on some of the pieces depending upon the piano, the acoustics of the room, and musical considerations.

ABOUT THE COMPOSERS

**Amy Beach** (1867–1944) was an American pianist and composer whose musical gifts were recognized at a very young age. Many considered her the most important female composer in the United States during her lifetime. Married to a physician, she used the name Mrs. H. H. H. Beach on many of her compositions.

**Carl Czerny** (1791–1857) was an Austrian pianist, teacher, and composer. He taught only talented students and devoted the remainder of his time to composition and arrangements of classical works. He published almost 1,000 compositions during his lifetime with numerous other manuscripts left unpublished.

**Anton Diabelli** (1781–1858), an Austrian publisher and composer, wrote numerous piano duets. He was the publisher of Schubert's first printed works. An experienced musician, piano teacher, and composer, he was able to respond to musical trends of the day. Consequently, his publishing company was a huge financial success.

**Theodor Kirchner** (1823–1903) was a German composer, organist, conductor, and pianist. He served as director of the Wurzburg Conservatory and also taught at the Dresden Conservatory. He wrote many character pieces for piano that are similar to those of Robert Schumann.

**Ignaz Moscheles** (1794–1870), a German, was a virtuoso pianist, teacher, and composer. He studied in Prague and Vienna, where he knew Beethoven. He and his piano student Felix Mendelssohn became very close friends. At the Leipzig Conservatory, he taught piano students from all over the world.

**Fritz Spindler** (1817–1905), a German pianist and composer, published more than 330 works. Most of these works were drawing room pieces and teaching music for piano. Other works included trios, sonatinas, two symphonies, and a concerto for piano.

**Igor Stravinsky** (1882–1971), a Russian composer, had a profound influence on the evolution of music in the 20th century. A prolific composer, he wrote works for the stage, orchestra, chamber music, vocal music, and piano music. He became an American citizen in 1945 and the United State Postal Service issued a two-cent stamp bearing his image in 1982.